Imagine the Glacier

poems by

Matthew Burns

Finishing Line Press
Georgetown, Kentucky

Imagine the Glacier

ACKNOWLEDGMENTS

Thanks to the editors of the journals where many of these poems first
appeared:

*Anderbo, Broad River Review, Caduceus, Camas, Cathexis Northwest Press,
Cleaver Magazine, decomP, ellipsis…, Georgetown Review, Graze, Heron Tree,
The Lake, Lime Hawk, Memoir (and), North American Review, Posit, Pretty
Owl Poetry, Quiddity, Raleigh Review, RHINO, Rock & Sling, Sediments,
Sweet Tree Review, Upstreet Magazine, and Young Ravens Literary Review.*

Publisher: Leah Huete de Maines
Editor: Christen Kincaid
Cover Art: Michael Conlin / ConlinStudios.com
Author Photo: Christina Ditmar (Good Love Photo) @goodlovephoto
Cover Design: Elizabeth Maines McCleavy

Order online: www.finishinglinepress.com
also available on amazon.com

Author inquiries and mail orders:
Finishing Line Press
P. O. Box 1626
Georgetown, Kentucky 40324
U. S. A.

Table of Contents

For Jill, who's been there every step of the way.

"It's a magical world, Hobbes, ol' buddy…
… let's go exploring!"
—Calvin and Hobbes, 12/31/95

When it is Cold and I Smell Roses

And here, friends, is what I believe
to be pure faith: the red squirrel,
small and nimble in the cold,
back arched and holding her fat
belly out of the snow as she
makes her way back to the leaf-ball
nest high in the bare white oak
now gone back to white again.

I believe in the flat mat of clouds
that holds everything together
and presses down on the garbage bins
I have taken out to the curb,
and on the pregnant squirrel,
her swollen teats, the warm pups
in her full belly that may not
make it past their first hard week.

I do not want children and I have
only recently come to want a dog,
but in this air, in the pink wrap
of rose and snow, I think I may be
able to do something that requires
more than I believe I have in me.

December

Think of the frost
That will crack our bones eventually.
—Tom Hennen, "Love for Other Things"

I will, and I will
Walk into the morning
Light falling like snow: a flurry:
Life. Cold is and I am.

Tell me something other.
I will walk away, leaving:
Everything I am.

They say (they and I,
I say and lie) when one is
Inhaled by avalanche
The bright fire of life is
Stoked in wind and
A great black night.
It is night,

Now; I am alive.
The frost will do: crack,
Cry: a sky of bones
Ready to alight on my lying.

I am thinking of the morning
Light, but it is far and
Unrelieving.

My bones are alive,
Flying for now, for tonight.

The Sharp Air

The river I don't know
rumples over its rocks
and carries anything
that falls in—silt and brush,

a tumbleweed blown
from ten miles away.
The river is clear and silent.
When I crouch at its trembling lip

or pitch the rare flat stone across its skin,
I am looking for something
to carry me, not away but up.
Like the chickadee's call to its mate

that goes *bay-bee* and *bay-bee*
until she calls back with same
and they go on beside the river
so it carries this, too, away;

so that it unwinds and eddies,
like the silt of missing,
into the air; the sharp air,
carrying everything it can hold.

One-Eyed Snowy Owl by the Side of the Tracks

It is bright, late day,
and we are neither
invisible nor silent, the way
we should be now.
The ballast, like the days
up here, grows colder
in silent weight
and someone—a worker
tired of trespass
and only looking to move
into the lonely night
with no hassle—
might be along
to shoo us away.
I know you are afraid:
that eye, its wide gold disc,
left me only when you tottered
from one frost-iced tie,
northward to the next, as if
you knew north
was the direction of home.
Those wings, fingers
of stranded flight, laid
splayed as beseeching hands
against the steel rail.
And when I finally reached
to cup and lift your small,
feathered mass,
the bright day opened
into a forest of white.
There is no one here but us,
and I am looking north.
Let whatever that will
come toward us come today
and either take us in
or throw us back
to the unflinching woods.

The Pig, the Hog

Dawn so cold
that a fat pig, a hog,
was found alive
but frozen on its side
to the ground

that must have been mud
when it laid its pink bulk
down last night. We walked
around and tried to figure
just how to free it
without too much blood
or suffering—no pry bars
or tow hooks; the ground
too hard for shovels.

And the pig, the hog,
that rooted largeness
exhaled into the morning
but did not struggle
or cry out. It laid and blinked
its tired eyes when we stroked
its head and put feed
to its warm snout that sniffed
for the rising day.

We waited and when
it finally stood, unlatched
from the cold stone returning
to mud under a higher sun,
there was the clean outline
of its whole body left behind.

I put my hand in that memory
of the pig and could feel
each minute of her long night
pressing back and I was scared.

Great Northern

To my wife, on the train

I should tell you
about the view I have,

of the way I can see
from my seat

the headlamp of the engine
shining into the night

ahead, of the slice of black
sky appearing above the cut,

around the bend of track
that bends above the Snohomish

that, in turn, bends
through the northern reaches

of the Cascades
like an endless white string

or strand of hair laid down
among rocks and trees.

We have been here before,
but not in the night, in winter;

not wrapped in the black
weight of mountains

that makes us feel alone.
I feel alone and I

should tell you this.
This would erase that weight

and leave its gray ghost
to sit beside me,

on the other side of the window
like a reflection

dragged across the last
visible piles of snow.

I should tell you all of this
and that, as we roll through

the giant, unknowing night,
through some crossing

in Glacier or Whitefish or Libby
and you are lit

by a passing streetlight
or the highbeams from some car

waiting, heavy with loneliness,
for the train to pass,

I can see for miles
and miles ahead.

Home for the Holidays

The creek: a crack
cloven
and black
though a snow-
coated field.
   The field:
a haze
white among
line after line
of knives of high
ridge and high ridge
and high
ridge.

I want you
to know
what it means
to come
   home
in the cold

and meet that old
life like the first
time you hold
a child.
   This life:
mine: flowing
along some long line

already cut
and winding
through an old field
I know
I've walked in
   before.

My Father's Son

I drink too much and bite my nails
and the snow blows in gales down the street;
I hear it when everyone is asleep.

If it weren't the cold, then it would be the wind
that screams. We all complain.
The winter is forever cold; the summer,

too hot then never enough.
It could always be better and worse.
We are miserable and thankful, hateful

and weeping alone in the night
at the simple heartbreak of everything
that surrounds us—the wind in the high pines;

a coyote calling out; the sky punched-through
with planes and stars; the recognition
that the deep black morning's 2:15 to Las Vegas

and the pinpricks of Orion are hunting
the same impossible things:
certain bounty, peace of surety.

When I wake to piss, somewhere
between early dark and early light,
dehydrated, unsteady, this little red house

surrounds me. The night, and a life
that has fallen in this miraculous bounty,
surrounds me. The snow blows

in some white hate down the street,
but I am close enough to sleep
to hear nothing but the warmth of everything safe.

Working Late

In absentia uxorem

We decided: it is you
who must go first.
You said so, years ago,
and I will eventually find
the thin road leading to acceptance
of that. I can sleep every night
under the mantle of assurance
that says: the forest is larger
than I can conceive,
and there are train tracks
winding their iron lines
into every lonely corner
of someplace we've never been.
        Or, more simply:
When you are gone,
I will be too. Long gone.
One disappearance demands
another, a balance.
When you leave, leave knowing this.
But tonight is filled
by nothing but wind.
That is how it will be then;
I know: void and vacuum
replaced by the constant dragging-
through of something familiar
but still, somehow, transient,
always. Some memory I create
so I can sleep beneath
a mantle of trees and stars.
I am saying this:
we cannot hold onto anything
beyond whatever we have
right now. And even then,
whatever we call *missing*
is just a circle around a hole:

the thing that defines the thing
that is gone.
It is nearly ten o'clock
on a Thursday night in February,
and there is a whole forest of wind
winding its iron way
through every little crevice
in this building we call home.
I am alone, for the first time
in nearly twenty years,
and feel like I am disappearing
into some dream of trees
that refuse to move for anything.
That makes no sense, I know;
there is no way to make sense
of this. This is someplace
we've never been,
and I cannot find my way
for want of your voice to guide me.

Nocturne

My wife, making dinner
sings along to a song on the radio
and cuts onions
and sets them in the dutch oven
I bought her one day
in June fifteen years ago.
It has been that long

and I know it. There is snow
outside, but it isn't cold
tonight. I hear the knife
work its sharp way through
whatever she cuts
and I think of my bloody finger

healing beneath a bandage of gauze.
Four days ago
I detipped my left index
slicing clementines
in the winter night.
I am healing more

and more every day, but
when it hurts, it hurts most
at night: a throbbing.
It matches my heartbeat in bed:
a few seconds I count off
and then fall toward sleep.

When I sleep, I dream
of the disc of skin
that shot into the snow,
a white comet
of flesh, a tail of blood.
I dream of the knife.

When I wake, afraid

and sweating in the night,
I think of her smooth cut
through the onions,
through the white flesh
that yields to the blade and edge.

I think of the song
coming through the air,
invisible as night, and her soft voice
running along beside this verse,
the one that follows, the next
and the next, until the music
and its old melody fades.

Shovel and Rasp

I said I'd be in the garage
with a drink, putting an edge
on the new shovel to hone
the rounded steel, *blading* it
the way I'd read one should
before and after every season.

I bought a rasp and a file, too,
for just this and every moment
that settles into the hollow of rest
before work or after, when there is time
to sit in a chair and hold things gently.

The ground is frozen a foot deep
but the burrs of metal settling
onto the dust of snow in the bare yellow
bulblight will end up in the soil
come March, just when the eager
black earth can be turned over again
to steam in the new sun. And then,

in the early dusk months later,
I will sow flecks of blade again
deep for the long winter ahead,
with hands stronger and rougher
than they are now. (My hands ache
for a strength they have not known.)

But I stack another empty
on the top shelf in the corner
and sit down in the lawn chair
left open to look to the stubbly fields
that unroll in dark hills
away from me, into the past
where every last son has tried
to dig his way out.

Tonight, I am the last
one, with steel slivers in my palms,
waiting for the ground to thaw.
Tonight, I am the field.
Tonight, I am shovel and rasp;
the blade and its bright new edge.

Watermelons

If I ever forget what to live for
and go out to meet that bony man
of despair who sits on a bar stool
in the back of my mind, nursing a bottle
of cheap booze and playing solitaire

to kill time until some stupid thing
calls out to him and he can finally
toss back the rest of his glass
and sidle up to whatever may be left
of my weary heart;

if that ever happens and I forget
all there is to live for,
show me a slow-motion film
of my love licking her lips and saying
the word "watermelons."

Show me just one grainy frame
of that reel—preferably the one
where she has just the pink tip
of her tongue peeking out
from between her teeth as she lolls
through the word's slow, penultimate *L*—

show me that fraction-of-a-fraction
of a second and I will know
that every horrible, grief-ridden thing
in this world can be dulled
to something bearable.

And I will pour Despair another drink,
say I'm sorry for making him get up,
send him back to the bar with a freshly-
shuffled deck, and let him play another
thousand hands while I ask for that film
to be run again, please, just one more time.

How to Go Home

Head North.
Forget the warehouses
held up by planks and the railroad
tracks coated black with coal; or,
rather, do not hate them the way you did
when they bent into you, tall and long

in their reach, deep too, dust under
your nails, grease in your veins. Look
at the rivers in their swell; they have nothing
against you; they do not care; not about the time
in '89, in January, when you almost drowned,
setting old tires on fire and sliding them

across the ice like cheap comets—your weight
too much, the stink of melting rubber, the heat
too much, and then the cold that felt hot
for a good minute once you were in,
neck-deep—and they still do not care
about the thousand small rocks you've kicked

from the trestle nor the heavy ones you heaved
at the coffins when they floated south after May
rains washed them from their plots, pulled them
away to new grounds downstream;
the river does not even remember you. Keep
in mind: the firehouse and the creamery

and the public pool from first grade
all do not know your name,
even if they're still there, holding on to the ground
beneath, the ground holding on, too,
the way everything here holds on: desperately
so it will not be ripped away.

Behold, be held. Stand on the hills,
sit in the parking garage, lie down

in the bottle return at the grocery store,
it all points to the same sure thing:
it will be waiting when you come back.
All of it.

To the One Student Who Shook My Hand After Class Today

When I told everyone
the story of my friend who OD'd,
you were first cleaning your nails
with a pocketknife
and then re-lacing your work boots.

And when I said
I had spent too many years
drinking too much
because I felt like that was the only way
to commit words to a page,

you held the glowing psalm
of that phone like gospel
in your palms: penitent, silent.
I say these things and hope
to be alive before you.

These are conspiratorial words:
You do not want to be here;
I know. Today, neither did I.
But we do what we must
in order to move on.

And therein lies the balance
of everything. Whatever the reason
you hung behind, minutes
and then minutes more after
every screen glanced at beneath a desk

said it was time to move on
to whatever was scheduled or happening
after our little class
on this snowy Thursday afternoon,
I felt like it must be grounded

in either spite or despair: a joke

between you and friends; a rampart
against caring enough, too much.
But now I think, maybe, it was
a sudden mirror held up

to something still raw and familiar.
Maybe it rose in some font of loss
buried inside you, but I hope not.
You are too young for despair.
Save that in some secreted stockpile

for later, when you are surrounded by nothing
but a blizzard of love.
Balance—*listen*—matters here.
Here: a confession:
I was immediately suspicious.

And here: one more: I was thankful.

Rhubarb

The poison lives only in the leaves,
thick with instant bitterness to warn you,
and my Polish grandmother said
this was to kill off the lazy ones,
the stupid ones, the ones who wanted
things handed to them, who couldn't
find it in themselves to dig.

And planting it told everyone
you didn't mind dirt under your nails,
that you knew life was hard work
if you did it right. So she grew more
than the whole family could eat.

By May, her narrow terraced backyard
in the city's First Ward was a lapping sea
of palm-sized leaves; by June,
a solid ruff of green, a pruning knife's
hooked blade biting through the stalks
with a flick of her wrist and a quick snap.

The one time I tried this I sliced deep
into my thumb knuckle at first swipe.
We were both red inside,
me, the rhubarb.
That's the stuff I didn't really think about
at ten, how everything bleeds;
how everything must die somehow—
the stupid ones poisoned, the hard workers
heart-worn and wrecked.

We ate the rhubarb raw, stripped
of all its leaves. Dipped in sugar
it still lingered bitter on our tongues
as a little inoculation against the worst
of what was yet to come.

Street Confession

All the way down Main
this morning, toward the store
for a paper and apples,
every light was red.

Let me be forgiven
for running them all
just to stay with the lone crow
that flew in front of me
for ten blocks.

And the fingers of its wings
never moved, just lay splayed
out to shape the wind that blew
us east beside the low river
that is already beginning to stink.

For surety of the black beak
I have forsaken the stop signs
and trees half-wrapped in tinsel
shivering back to last Christmas,
I have renounced the used-car lots
where I've watched the same nine vans,
for as long as I can remember,
get marked down every year.

And I think I'm learning
how to be sorry, old town,
for every crack I've made
about those trucks and rust,
for the crumbs of pity I heap
on your broke-down rent-to-own
and dollar stores, and especially
for the splash of laughter
in your bars and Sunday-morning
puddles someone left there
the night before

in a little circle of themselves
returning to these streets.

Streets, forgive me and hold me
as the wind holds the crow
whose feet hide folded,
whose beak points east,
whose wings do not flap
when the dapple of shade
and light between every corner
runs over its dark
dark-blue back
like absolution.

Townes

I'm another year gone
toward I don't even know what,
and it nearly hit sixty today.

It's barely March,
but dad sent me a picture
of the cat watching a deer

nurse its early fawn
beneath the bird feeder
and wrote a story

about the whole thing.
It read like everything
that's ever made me weep.

I'll sleep on that tonight,
that and a song I've heard
a hundred times

playing like a cat or fawn
across the field of a day
that rose in early warmth

two weeks before spring
was even a dream.
I'm another year gone.

It nearly hit sixty today;
they say tomorrow
could be even warmer.

Calving

When a cow gives birth,
they call it *calving*, too.
It happens most often
in the morning: sunrise, later.
Black cows dropping smaller
cows: wet, slippery.
The sun, unraveling,
warms both. The sun,
breaking over the mountains.

Sunrise doesn't reach
the waterline until late.
It only dusts the topmost
points of the ice.
The mountains in the east
keep us in shade.
Blue shade, blue ice cut-
through with a different blue.
They call it *calving*
when the ice breaks free, falls.

Sea the color of sky
rolls in against the outflow.
Both wash the black shore
clean, smooth as birth.

Imagine the Glacier

"Anchor me in ice"
                    —Bell Witch, *Mirror Reaper*

and its crystalline weight
mile-thick and memory
of pebbles beneath
chattering lines
into bedrock
a quarter-million years ago
like the unheard hum
of some under-song
when what we're listening to
fades out toward some
somber reversal of
songbirds in predawn:
a retraction
of life ablossom.

Imagine the drone
that sounds for everything
like some great weight
poured leaden onto bone
as an echo, remnant, forgotten
hymn sung to the long ago
granite and lost until the now
of an inexorable carving-out.

A pair of foals

lies in the field
as if dead: flat out,
legs pointed
toward the sun
that has just broken
over the frosted hills,
forehead blazes touching
like pursed white lips.
       I saw them

breathe together,
breaths becoming breaths
becoming whatever
breaths become
once they've left
and moved out
into the wide ranch
of sky around us.
       They moved together

and moved the dust
and I moved away
toward the small
chores that pulled me
on like a team of horses.
Later, coming out
of the Safeway
with a loaf of bread
and some apples,
I thought of them,
cozy foals:
       that young couple

in the parking lot,
at five o'clock
on a Tuesday
afternoon in May,

sitting on the hood
of a pick-up,
their foreheads together
ablaze and breathing
their teenage love
into each other,
            while the wind

drew up its sleeves
and blew dust
and cherry blossoms
down from the trees.

The Border

"We have no way of indicating where
one location ends and another begins..."
—The Onion, 3/25/15

or whatever belongs
anywhere. We have somehow,
in haste and hubris, walked
into a deep night.
Right now I am reaching

for some tree or signpost
or mile marker that sticks
in the heavy dark.
If this is what
tomorrow will be,

then let me fall
into some lost stupor.
The line I drew
across the map of my life
last night has gone to dust,

and I am now nothing
but the sum of every assumption
and guess made the dark.
I am dumb.
I will confide in you,

my friend, my concierge,
my brother conspirator:
whatever meant something
last night now means little
beyond the menial and greedy.

Don't listen to me;
it is raining, and I am filled
with the white space

of erasure as sheep
are filled with grass in spring.

That is: wholly. Here.
Let me say what I think
I mean: It looks like rain
on the road tonight—
there is rain on the road tonight.

Virga

I am cutting the sleeves off of every shirt I own
and drinking warm wine from a chipped jam jar.

The thunder and heat lightning that breaks over the ridge
is thick June's gnashing of teeth. *This* and *this* and *this*

I point to in the dark is me trying to say we should never
be far away from whatever has grown to be called home.

I am, we are far away from home and lit in intervals
by the orange and blue light from ten thousand feet up.

It stands our fine hairs on end and runs down my arm,
bare shoulder to bare wrist to trembling hand and glass.

And the air is warm and tastes like concentric spheres
of sky pressed into a pair of ions that sit on my lips

like invisible shards of glass, cut that skin, and move
to yours when we kiss and sweat under the ridge

suddenly lit and now suddenly dark again.

Relative Chronology

Understand time like this:
Ride a train west
through the wide amber heart
of the country
and watch the sun hover
unmoving for half a day
like a great tern
facing the wind, lifted
by its fingered wings
to hang in the sky
on the magic wires of flight.

At some point
between the place we've left
and the place we're going,
when we counter
the persistent spin of the earth,
there will be a second that
does not go by.

Even if I cannot do the math to prove it,
I want to believe
in that riddle of the man
who walked away from the rising sun
and kept his shadow the same
length all day.

I am earthbound and tired
and it might not yet be noon
in the big rutted country running by
but I think I may have learned
what it means
to want nothing more
than a stretch of level track
and a second,
when we finally stop,
to shade my eyes

with a crow's feather
and look back into the light.

On the Bear Canyon Trail

Is it "lu*pine*,"
like the tree—the spruce

and fir; Scots, mountain,
and eastern white:

green spires that run
into the winter night

and hold; or is it
"lu*peen*": like a hammer

of flower, not pounding
but steady tapping: a rhythm,

some rounding out
of the steel that ends up

poured across every day
spent somewhere

that does not care
about these things?

       I still don't know.

On the Bear Canyon trail
in Washington—an hour

west out of Yakima,
where no one goes—

there is a ridge
that lifts itself over the valley

like a rapture
of calming hands,

like manna for the sad
and aching. I do not know

what to call them, but you can
find those flowers there.

I remember: I ached
and was drawn away,

into that wild. There were
high pines and flowers,

the leg of an elk
some vulture left

dangling in a tree.
There was that lost

hammer of life beating
out a rhythm to carry me—

a tool, some machine.
It rang out (believe me)

in peals like petals
rising to meet the day.

This Valley

"...call it our life."
—Levine, "Our Valley"

Let's not, and instead call it someone else's.
Not ours but whoever fell like the fog,
like the smoke here. And what of those
who stuck, pushing taproots into the hardpan
and dust? In spite of everything everyday
that said *Get up; just go,* I remember that
kind of safety. I can't forget: this isn't our land,
no matter what depth of forest or rise of mountain
into the cold elevations beyond Rimrock Lake
we run to; it belongs to people we'll never be,
not that way, not the way red maple and hemlock
mountains rolling down from Maine to North Carolina
were, not the way the cold Atlantic will always be.
But if these mountains don't speak the language
of ocean, I want no part of them. What mountain
doesn't with ghosts of coral and shell at 9000 feet?
We have settled in this valley for now, and there
is a scent of smoke on the wind again.
Again it makes its way inside us.

Black Mass

Bulk and weight,
        like something tossed
        into the field
after every last scrap of use
        was exhausted:
        black mass,
dead cow, today the sun is high
        and you are rotting
        and I am driving home
from a ten-dollar haircut.

When I get back,
        I know one of the few people
        I love as much as life
will be untying her shoes
        or chopping onions
        or some other routine,
loving thing that moves the day forward
        another two steps
        toward the mass of night
where we will lie together

under the weight of covers
        that lie under the weight
        of that blooming field of sky
where everything ends up.
        Good night, mass of cow.
        Rotten pile in the field
down the road, good night.
        I know we will lie there,
        waiting and praising sleep
when it finally descends.

A Burning

High dusk in the high desert: hills
oxidized, the sun fights to burn
through the quintillion motes of smoke
      carried on the imperceptible wind
      from a whole family of wildfires

that appeared in one long, dry night
like so many wanton visitors
      and their ashy baggage.
      We all look up at this ruby—

no, this candy orb—no,
this: full-crystalline bauble blown
      of nameless minerals. Just heat
      and color and light sent: a gift

of unwrapped blades. We can hardly see
or cough. We can hardly think to do anything
      but stare, unsure, and look away
      so the scalding ghost of the sun

can burn still in the backs of our eyes.
The smoke is so thick that, love,
      I can feel every mote
      of your frightened breath

tumble like dry waves against my ear.

Friscalating Dusklight

We know nothing is real in this made-up night.
The runaway son doesn't really love his adopted sister
who's secretly been sleeping with his childhood best friend,

the drug-addled cowboy author
whose mediocre first book was, he now admits,
"written in a kind of obsolete vernacular."

None of them even exist.
Nor does the long-absent patriarch
who, having been evicted from his hotel,

now fakes a case of stomach cancer
so he can return to the family brownstone
and meddle in his abandoned wife's new romance.

There is no widower brother
compulsively obsessed with safety;
and the mice he bred as a child:

nothing but white spots on a white page.
We know this with all our hearts and do not care.
In the quiet snowfall of the projector's frames,

this is all we need to know: we will laugh and cry
and feel some strange relief when it all ends in the cemetery.
Then we will talk through the long list of credits

and move out of the usher-held doors into the rising night,
where our wide eyes, still dilated from the theater's darkness,
will again need time to adjust to life on the outside,

where we all know the million ways love can fail,
where even the friscalating dusklight hanging on after the show
is more than either of us can take.

Sailor's Delight

Matthew 16:2–3

When I kiss my wife
in the kitchen or the garden,

when she comes down from upstairs
where she has been reading

or whatever, I kiss her forehead
and put a hand on her cheek

because this is how you live
in another after twenty years.

I'm four decades deep. Listen.
This is how you live:

skin against skin on bone:
warm and needy. The sun

is high and bright today,
and the sky will be red tonight.

You know what they say:
"sailor's delight,"

so I will push my thin lips
against her head, wait

for the day to rise,
and pray the morning sky is gray.

Gray Dress

I want her to ask me to pull the zipper
on that one gray dress she bought

last summer in a fit of wardrobe formality
after wondering aloud one morning

to the hollow maw of the closet
why she has nothing nice to wear.

Now she struggles with that long
white ribbon tied like a lost hair

into the pull, the one that exists
for no other reason than to reach

over the pale shoulder so a wearer
can wear it even if she is alone,

getting ready to go out and thinking
of the night. But what do I know?

I only want to be asked. I only want
to feel, in the bones of my hand,

that chatter of teeth click together
up the pale road of her spine,

because far away there is suffering
I cannot comprehend.

Bomb blast and torture unpeel flesh
from ruddy muscle; floods of gray mud

fill the mouths of wailing children;
and women are being disappeared

into the unloving night, into horror

beyond measure. And the next day

after it all, the fact that someone
must wear some new life like a skin,

too tight now, always, is crippling;
and this happens, too.

So when she faces away from me,
the bare closet bulb like an interrogator's

lamp across her shoulder and the mouth
of the zipper wide like a wail,

I am here to do the little I can
so she will not be afraid:

my lips by her ear, my hand
on the small of her back.

The Inheritance of the Farmer's Grown Son

Here is hot, deepest July,
when everything will unfurl in supple joy.

Here is the cattail and the oak in the sun;
the tall dill and corn my father's hands dug
into the earth, all now rooted strong as rope knots.

The loam then pebble then clay
gave way beneath his nails in spring,
when the blade of a clear night's frost
still lurked at the cloche-edge until noon.

Here is the blackness of soil rich in rows.
That was months ago.

Now he rises from the cool nimbus
of elm shade blooming in the late
late-afternoon only when he must.

Already riddled with the plague of age,
he carries marbles of ache in every joint
and must work hard
to catch a bat trapped in the house
or unravel a game from the radio dial.

Still—and this is what I will take with me—
his hands are quick to pull up their old tangle
of roots and point over the roiling tops of trees
gone purple in the sun's last light, to say:

There, the stars!
The stars; and, look: the moon!

We End

In the twin black ghosts
of tires on a road, thick
lines that reek of panic
and squeal left after someone
stomped on the brakes,

in the dark, in the wake
of the sudden appearance
of gold eyes in the night—
a dog or fox or coyote running
from one culvert to another

in the black of a desert unlit
by streetlight or any moon
we have seen—I think
there may be a lesson:
We end before we know.

The thirty-foot lines
of rubber burnt into the street,
and the ghost of whatever
spilled itself sometime this week,
run under my tires, under

my feet pushing me north,
pushing me toward a house
where someone I love is waiting,
gold eyes like candles
in the falling night.

We end and I know this
and I will drive until
there is nothing left to do
but push my foot into the floor
and stop, squealing, and yes,

finally coming to rest

beside a culvert that runs
with water clear and clean
and cold enough to carry me
into some new beginning.

John Prine

"...And I dream of her always / even when I don't dream."

He sounds like the desert
northwest to me,
every night, somehow, still.

Central Washington,
if you've never been, is hot
then cold then hot then something
vaguely resembling February
before the wildfires light and burn
into the round red orb of late-summer,
then lonely.

For two blank years, I drove to work
or to the store for beer or to the quiet,
holy train yard on a Sunday morning
to write the name, the one I've said
to fewer than a dozen people,
on as many cars that would hold
and carry it to someplace I believed
I would never go to or return,
and played "Christmas in Prison"
on my car radio, no matter what season,
and thought of the sweet hot brush fire
of my wife who came with me.

She was home, and I was not.
That was not home, but she was there.
I still feel bad about that. And I don't
usually sing other peoples' songs,
because I can barely sing my own, but
there is one lonely line that keeps rumbling
like some little freight train
making the same run
through the high desert night,
and, for the love of everything,
I can't get it out of my head.

What We Talk About When We Talk About Weather

for my parents, after calling long-distance

And, yes, we miss you
and trains and maples and diners
that open early and diners that close
right after lunch; we miss a house
we've lost in the mist of distance.

And yes, we often talk long
into the night of rivers that merge
in smooth confluence beside the railroad
that has sat in its mute ballast
for much longer than a century.

The quiet on the line is not boredom
but rather a hollow where silence settles
next to a measure of grief where both
lie down together. They hold one another
through the nights that freeze

and the days that melt.
Now, when I hear myself say "back East,"
what comes out is more than just
the right side of a map on a table.
There is root and foothold.

There are low clouds and chill and everyone
I manage to love. The hills and valleys
of the Northeast, where they all stuck
and found one another between rivers

and trees, and came together,
like rain in the gutter, like frost on grass
or leaves or whatever laid in quiet
on the ground in the morning.
I know you have been asleep

for some time; dawn left you
hours ago and these days the night
comes on fast. But in this western desert
it is almost dusk, and there isn't a diner
or train around for miles, and it is cold here, too.

To the Groundhog My Father Wants to Drown

but doesn't and instead
drives out to the country to set free:

If you know what stars are,
thank them tonight as you're curling up

in that new den you've spent
the warm autumn afternoon digging

into this new land far, far away
from the backyard and garden you've been

marauding all summer.
There is no Bibb lettuce out there, I know,

no rows of radish or deep-
rooted carrot to purloin and fill your fat body.

There is no fifty-five-gallon drum
filled with rainwater, either, so think hard

on the balance in that. Out there,
what must be some wild equivalent of a thousand

groundhog-miles away
from the suburban patch my dad cultivated

for a few dozen tomatoes, a few
late-summer salad's-worth of green and orange,

you'll last years. Goldenrod
and Queen Anne's Lace will sustain,

believe this. You cannot understand
or even hear me, I know, but know you are as lucky

as the stars whose light makes it

to this humble, wild spot in just a million lifetimes

more than you or I can begin
to create in our little, animal minds. So,

when tonight opens above you
as it opens above everything else, let's make a deal:

if you will, I will; we can, far apart and full
of miraculous luck, take it all in, together.

For a Morning in October

The paper says:
in the folded and unfeeling
quilt of the mind,
memory sticks
like a burr pulled

from the prickly thicket
of experience.
And I think
how ideal this image is
for such a morning

when the neighbors' baby
cries its long whooping cry
at the sound of a dropped pot
and the blue jay shouts
from some close maple.

How ideal it is
for this hour when every
sound must be either
gloriously blessed or
painful: that carbine shot

of wind-thrown door
and the last bleating
ambulance call of the night.
These are the noisy burrs
of memory for a morning

in October.
Their little hooked hands,
for reasons I'll never really
understand, have decided
to hold tight

to that heavy woolen quilt,

the one I've been sewing
together for years
without having learned
one single locking stitch.

Heroin Sonnet

"Mom accused of injecting daughter with heroin..."
—Reading (PA) *Eagle*

Dear child, little petal of my flower, I do not know
If life is anything more than this: a dream
Awake but not. Trust me. In the white cut of day, a seam
Cut through our lives—yours and mine—this can show
Every little flaw in what everyone calls *living.*
Tonight, when I hold your fist and place the needle to
Your arm left trembling under the touch of my fingers gone blue,
Left blunt and swollen with—trust me—the want of giving,

My love—only love, trust me—will unfurl like flowers and grace.
Or, if not grace, then something you have never touched:
Rest and peace and calm: white petals: the hushed
Pleasure of stupor, of daze. Trust me. This is the pure base
Hidden under everything you know. Somewhere interred beneath,
Inside your wild, flowering mind, I know this white truth hides
Nascent, like blossom and proliferation—roots of every lie,
Every dream: alive. A rest, some peace. Trust me. Trust me. Trust me.

An Orchard Alight

There is an orchard
burning after being relieved
of all its limbs
      and simple trimmings.
In the morning before
you arrive, a hired hand
(undocumented) piles
      those shorn arms, lost producers,
      lost hosts,
head-high and waits
to light the whole thing alive,
a little, again.
      A mile away, maybe more,
      the heat rises, is as visible as life.
You are alive as you were
last night; and even today,
in the high morning rising higher
      like light or fire
      (that old hired hand),
you have already arrived
at the wide life that was blooming
and breaking off
      in hot, wild relief.

Instructions for an Elegy to Ginger, the Chicken

The hawk ate today, at least.
Tell your son this when you put him to bed.

Tell him this is the way of a world
that—in spite of his drawn-out attempts
and sleepless nights spent staring out
at the stars or, like tonight, at the low
pink clouds that portend snow and feel
like thick blankets—is something
of which he can never, never make sense.

Tell him a hawk will now survive
the black and pink night, will roost
warm and full, the way we all hope
to go to bed when it is cold.

Tell him, gently, like a mother,
that the white pile of feathers
that two mornings ago was a chicken
is now an altar to both loss
and buying time, to staving-off
and persistence and the bloody
life we cannot see for want
of a night's sleep, even as it drifts
across the back yard, the wind
carrying it away, the wind
for no reason beyond itself.

Tell him this and say *good night, love;*
good night my little hungry beast.

The equation of tonight

goes something like this:
Let A = the dark
of last evening where
8:30 felt like the heavy end
of everything that matters.
And B can then stand
for that weight of sleep

denied in the white glare
of doubt rising like dawn
from your tired mind.
Take the square root of that
product and hang it in effigy
over the denominator that is day
upon day upon day here.

If X is to equal anything,
it is fatigue. Those who know
the intimacies of mathematics
say there is incomprehensible
beauty in it all. That the way
variables align and factor out
is tantamount to grace.

That faith, if it is worth anything,
is a whole string of numbers
balancing into zeroed-out
perfection, like the lights
clicking off and the dark,
the holy dark, descending
in its glorious weight.

After Lines by Wei Ying-wu, Misremembered

In my office library, the morning cold,
I suddenly think of a mountain guest...
    —"Sent to a Master of Way in the Utter-Peak Mountains"

In my awful library, the moving cold,
I suddenly think of a mountain goat,

miniature, tripping its way over bookstacks
before returning home to its fresh sedge and stone.

I long to carry that small thing,
holding it like a fetish in my palm, my pocket;

but every peak is miles to the west,
all stories of my having been there, unread.

On the Night Before My Wife Quits Her New Job

I imagine you rode it
like some non-stop red-eye
from Newark to Seattle:
enclosed and claustrophobic, black
windows over an overcast sky.

If there were stars, we missed them all.
I was gone beneath a quilt
of wine and warmth, enwrapped.

A night of nothing but thought
is the longest one, I know, but
we had both heard it for weeks:
the winter night and every fiber
of your heart whispering *Go.*

In my sleep, I thought it was just
the radiators' hiss. That prescient warmth
meant nothing beyond another quilt upon me.

You must have wept
beneath the weight of sleep denied
and how to escape, like some trapped passenger
riding out a rerouted flight
that took you and left you laid over
in some tertiary-market airfield in Iowa
when you only wanted to get to the coast
to see the simple morning sun
cut through the fog above the seaside cliffs
on a faraway and silent western shore.

Ghosts

The fog in
my throat:
palpable
zero—zero
being nothing
but, like
the past:
still there
and affecting.

Breath of
sky—my
visible breath
both unraveling
from and back
into grumbling
lungs.

Exhale, breath;
this is
where it ends,
round and
perfect.

The air:
perfect, equal
presence
on either
side of
my chest
in the morning.

Under the mass
of sky
laid low
and appearing
now is something,

finally,
we can see.

This must be
what welcomes us
as ghosts.

November

The wind rises like a hand
through my thin hair. A cat moves
like air through the backyard

and I think of my sister.
She has a new baby and I have a headache
and it is only Thursday.

This is what I mean when I say
I miss you, New York: this afternoon,
on the short, flat walk

between the two buildings I inhabit
every weekday, I pulled an oak leaf
the size of my hand from one

of the hundred arcing branches
that spread over just a small circle
of this whole brown western valley,

and made the mistake
of putting it to my face, hoping
there would be some memory there.

There was. The wind
that raises my hair is the same that raises
my sister's, her daughters', the trees gone

a dozen colors by now; there's no way
it can happen the other way around.
By the time it makes its way

across the mountains and plains
and rust-belt brownfields
the color of dead leaves,

they'll all have been asleep

for hours, wrapped around
one another in safe curls.

For the Dead Birds Found in Jim's Ceiling

I first think of their brittle, fragile skulls
when I hear of the rotten presence and wonder
if they look anything like the ones we saw
in that old knitting factory that, months after we broke in

and wandered every dark floor like wads of yarn
blowing in the miraculous breeze, were stripped
clean of flesh and feather and somehow bleached
skull-white. They must; a bird's skull is a bird's skull

no matter where it's found: the hard balloon of bone
riddled with holes, the point of beak still clinging
and true as flight. I am sorry you landed
in that dark space above my friend's head

and had to stay there until your fragile bodies met
forever—but who has the kind of say that says
how that will happen? If I did, let me tell you
long-gone pile of bones, featherless siblings,

it would be different—it will always be different—
as I know it would have been for you: there would be
an open sky; it would all be open and endless:
a fragile ceiling of sky; dark then, miraculously, bright.

The Snakes I Ran Over this Morning

After the little drumroll, that was my tires
flattening and then flattening again
your languid morning bodies,
       the hum of road reappeared.

It was as if there was a knock
and someone opened a door: there, all around,
was the sound of rubber and road touching
       and letting go and touching again,

fast as lovers in a backseat expecting
to be caught, to move me toward
a parking lot, the way tires must.
       Then horses in the field

I went past rubbed head-to-flank
and goats in the one behind laid
in their patches of grass and nibbled around
       out of boredom or hunger. The corn grew

dry and rattled in the rising wind that said
there was to be rain later. And there was rain
later and it fell because what else
       does it know to do beyond that?

And when, on the way home, I passed
what was left of your bodies—a shadow
under a three magpies pecking the wet road—
       it was just beginning to rinse away

into the culvert that is to be washed into,
the way everything out there is out there
to do one thing and do it beautifully.
       The road, the door, the horse,

and all that—that's what they do,
the same way I tell myself this

as I roll toward home through the early night
        coming on too fast to judge, speeding
        toward my tired, unsuspecting head.

To Potatoes

There is no cold,
root and white heart;
know this.

Starch fist unearthed,
do not tell the others:
you will be my last, best love.

You must know
we are from the same ground—
rich, silty ground—

and grow best
under a little damp,
enough to let us know

that, yes, there is something
holding us; there is us
and then more beyond that.

And the cold,
if we can call it that,
is our friend

and we should remember this
when the winter moves on us
like a gaunt vulture looking to feed.

We are not food,
you and I; we are
a weight in the belly

that feels warm
always, a heart
beneath a heart.

Whatever will eat us

will grow in warmth
and know the night

is not so long.
Sit in me and know
I feel you

and walk out
into the night—damp night,
scattered silt of stars—

and press my root hands
into the ground that moves
out to accommodate

and then back around
and takes me,
gratefully, in.

The Last Sunset in Barrow, Alaska

(two weeks after the election)

We'll subsist on spruce tea
      and satellite TV
for sixty days. Work will come,
and we'll look to the sky.
But day must rise
      in another dusk, and night
in some weird red light.
This town is a synonym
      for *carrier, hod*—something
to heft something heavier than us—
      and the night is a weight. We know.
It will be dark for days
and days that will feel
      like a sheet of ice
fifty meters deep. The wind
is a movie we've all seen;
      it weighs on everything.
The long dark is another
stack of bricks; a wide lead smock.
      But yet this: my chest
and belly: somehow, again,
warm and adrift. The TV is on,
      and the warm cup of the sun,
the day, will—it must,
I believe—come again.

In Winter

My God / I was tired of being a person.
    —Faith Shearin, "The Fox"

Snow thigh-deep is just dust
in the Cascade forest
a half-hour west;
I'm still trying to understand this.

The line of cars and ditched trucks
kill the white hours of night
in the shoulders
of mountain passes that the DOT guards

like some border crossing in eastern Europe
in the 50's, and the only things
in my car's trunk
are a map of Oregon and a bag of newspapers
I've been meaning to recycle since May.

That's the way it works, being ignorant
and staring ahead into the ever-
falling snow falling out of the unlit night.

It's like driving into the great white chest
of an animal that has laid
its whole tired weight
over the entire eastern side of the range:

like fur combed in lines, dense and endless, only
it must end at some point at elevation,
where the road rises above
the low clouds heavy with moisture and frost.

Love, I know you're scared, but we're not lost
yet; we'll go slow and sleep under trees
if we must. Let's keep going;
Listen: we're still alive, and we're not lost yet.

Five Practical Posthumous Uses for Human Bones

Phalanges, twenty, bleached: line the white mantle in winter, candelabra of loss and memory, gone fingers pointing up to a sky as unconcerned as the dirt. Picket fence, tiny pikes upon which you can impale everything unsaid.

Polished radius: weaker side, engrained with antipathy: shaped and sharpened: a bread knife or scythe. Grain of bone, grain of field. An arm to reach out and reap and bring toward some feast. Hunger will never cease, and we need to eat.

Sternum (shorn of ribs): doubtless: axehead, maul. Guard of heart for hardwood to be split—black birch, bur oak, something that burns long and hot. Shape a handle of hickory; hone and lash tight before the first strike.

Right patella: paperweight for utility bills, bundled junk mail, anything to be ground into soil.

Hyoid, broken, crushed, gilded: necklace, raw gold chain, worn slightly higher on the neck than comfortable: jaw beneath jaw, tacit mandible. Ghost of some gone voice healed after six weeks of silence. Tie just tight enough to bite into the throat's fine skin, to remember to speak again.

Born and raised in upstate New York, **Matthew Burns** is an Associate Professor, teaching creative writing and literature at SUNY Cobleskill. His poetry and essays have appeared in numerous national and international journals and his poem "Rhubarb" was the winner of the James Hearst Poetry prize from *North American Review*; others have been nominated for Pushcart Prizes and Best of the Net awards and appeared in *Camas, Cleaver Magazine, ellipsis…, The Lake, Paterson Literary Review, Posit, RHINO, Upstreet Magazine*, and others. Beyond creative work, Burns has served as editor for *Harpur Palate, Heron Tree,* and a special graffiti-themed issue of *Rhizomes: Culture Studies in Emerging Knowledge*. His scholarly work often focuses on the less-than-common and has included papers and courses on subjects as varied as Graffiti Linguistics, 20th-Century Music Subcultures, Hobos and Contemporary Transience, and Working Class Literature. He can be found online at *MatthewBurnsPoetry.com*.

www.ingramcontent.com/pod-product-compliance
Lightning Source LLC
Chambersburg PA
CBHW021157090426
42740CB00008B/1135